Jason Kahn

In Place

Errant Bodies Press:
Audio Issues Vol. 6

Zürich, Switzerland
July 4, 2014

Introduction

For many years before starting this project I'd been making environmental sound recordings in cities, in nature, at home with my family. In short, anywhere I could take a microphone. I used these recordings in room installations or incorporated them into compositions and musical performances as sound objects. But what increasingly occurred to me as I made these recordings was that something had eluded me. To bring these sound objects back to my studio and use them as material to work with was all fine and good, but what of the context I recorded these sounds in? What was the inherent nature of these places, vestiges of which still lingered on in the recordings? I began to feel that I was placing a wall between myself and these places with my microphones. The actuality of each situation I recorded in had escaped me. I'd thought that through recording I could get to the deeper meanings of a place, attempting to discern the consonance and dissonance of the many different spaces which constitute the notion of place. But in fact I failed to recognize all this while I was in the act of recording, concentrating not on the place but on the creative act of preserving a space of time as sound on my audio recorder.

The French phenomenological philosopher Maurice Merleau-Ponty believed that "both universality and the world lie at the core of individuality and the subject, and this will never be understood as long as the world is made into an object. It is understood immediately if the world is the field of our experience, and if we are making but a view of the world, for in that case it is seen that the most intimate vibration of our psychological being already announces the world, the quality being the outline of a thing, and the thing the outline of the world."[1] I wanted to move beyond the object I had created with my microphones. This didn't, however, detract from the enjoyment I had of later listening to the recordings I'd made, but I wanted to find a method to distance myself from this purely aesthetic practice and investigate the concepts of perception and presence as a means of fully comprehending the idea of a place and the myriad of spaces (social, physical, psychological, political) which produce it.

I then came across the book "Rhythmanalysis" by the French Marxist philosopher and sociologist Henri Lefebvre. Here Lefebvre succinctly formulated what I felt that I'd been missing. For him "no ear, no piece of apparatus could grasp this whole, this flux of metallic and carnal bodies. In order to grasp the rhythms, a bit of time, a sort of meditation on time, the city, people is required."[2] Lefebvre envisaged a new science, rhythmanalysis, where "the rhythmanalyst will listen to the world, and above all what are disdainfully called noises, which are said without meaning, and to murmurs, full of meaning – and finally he will listen to the silences.[3] He will be capable of listening to a house, a street, a town as one listens to a symphony, an opera."[4]

Where would it take me, to simply spend a day at a place, not doing anything but just being there? As another French philosopher, Gaston Bachelard, who preceded Lefebvre in the use of the term rhythmanalysis (and who in turn borrowed the term from its originator, the Portuguese philosopher and educator Lúcio Alberto Pinheiro dos Santos), wrote in his book "Dialectic of Duration," "pure consciousness will be revealed as the capacity for wasting and for watchfulness, as the freedom and the will to do nothing."[5] My intent in this work was simply the act of being somewhere without doing anything aside from concentrating on that place: its sounds, its smells, the pace of the day's light changing, the people coming and going, what Lefebvre called "the relations between everyday life and rhythms, which is to say the concrete modalities of social time."[6] All the furor and stasis which comprise a place. And I fathomed an implicit political imperative to this, which Lefebvre confirmed for me: "Without claiming to change life, but by fully reinstating the sensible in consciousness and thought, he [the rhythmanalyst] would accomplish a tiny part of the revolutionary transformation of this world and this society in decline. Without any declared political position."[7]

Much of my work, be it sound installations, musical compositions or pieces for radio, has been aimed at re-activating an interest in the world around us through sound. It seems that now, more than ever, people are not present in the world as they move through it. More and more they detach themselves and retreat into the relative safety of their cell phones, their tablets, their music players. There is much to avoid in the world around us – the noise of the cities with their dense trajectories of traffic and endlessly proliferating construction sites; the crowds of people; the pernicious bombardment of advertising images; and in practically every store or restaurant we go to, music or television brays incessantly.

But there is also much beauty in the world to be missed by not being conscious of it. And beyond this, the cultivated lack of awareness characterizes a growing apathy towards oneself and society in general. The composer and contrabassist Charles Mingus pointed out, "People are getting so fragmented, and part of this is that fewer and fewer people are making a real effort anymore to find out exactly who they are and to build on that knowledge. Most people are forced to do things they don't want to most of the time, and so they get to the point where they feel they no longer have any choice about anything important, including who they are. We create our own slavery."[8] Echoing this, Merleau-Ponty adds, "The task of radical reflection, the kind that aims at self-comprehension, consists paradoxically enough, in recovering the unreflective experience of the world, and subsequently reassigning to it the verificatory attitude and reflective operations, and displaying reflection as one possibility of being."[9] By falling out of touch with the world we also lose connection to ourselves.

Thus, I went back to the world, this time without my microphones to, in Lefebvre's words, "arrive at the concrete through experience."[10] In cities around the world I went to different places and spent a day there. I stayed anywhere from eight to twelve hours. And during this time I didn't do anything but be at these places. I didn't write down anything, I didn't take any photos, I had no cell phone with me, I didn't record any sounds and for the most part I didn't speak with anyone. I often sat at one location for several hours and then moved on to another position to experience a site from all its angles. I took breaks when I ate or used the restroom, but for the most part I was intent on being in a place, with all my body and soul. And after several hours I began to perceive the world opening around me, feeling what Lefebvre meant when he wrote, "Look around you at this meadow, this garden, these trees and these houses. They give themselves, they offer themselves to your eyes as in a simultaneity. Now, up to a certain point this simultaneity is mere appearance, surface, a spectacle. Go deeper. Do not be afraid to disturb this surface, to set its limpidity in motion. Be like the wind that shakes these trees. Let your gaze be penetrating, let it not limit itself to reflecting and mirroring. Let it transgress its limits a little." [10]

Like Merleau-Ponty, I believe that "to experience a structure [a place] is not to receive it into oneself passively: it is to live it, to take it up, assume it and discover its immanent significance." [11] And after these days of immersing myself in a place I was more often than not completely exhausted. I felt Lefbevre's words to the depths of my being, "He [the rhythmanalyst] will first have to educate himself (to break himself in or accept training), to work very hard therefore, to modify his perception and conception of the world, of time and the environment."[12] It was as if I'd emptied my entire being into these places, coming to a renewed understanding of the world and it of me. Merleau-Ponty captures the essence of this feeling when he writes, "I understand the world because there are for me things near and far, foregrounds and horizons, and because in this way it forms a picture and acquires significance before me, and this finally is because I am situated in it and it understands me."[13]

But beyond wanting to spend time in these places, I felt afterward that I also needed to somehow make sense of my passage there, resolving my thoughts and feelings through writing. Not as a simple point of reference, but, in Lefebvre's words, "In order not to isolate this present and in order to live it in all its diversity, made up of subjects and objects, subjective states and objective figures."[14] Sometimes I wrote these texts the day after, but often it took me longer to return to these places in my memory. My recollection of time spent in these places went beyond mental impressions. I felt as though each place had physically entered me, indelibly burned itself into my body. That I had fused with these places on a subconscious level. And by some small degree I had succeeded in raising my awareness of the world around me. As much as I'd given to these places with the energy of my attention they'd given back to me, becoming a process which Merleau-Ponty describes as "an atmospheric sound which is between the object and the body, a sound which vibrates in me as if I had become a flute or clock; and finally a last stage in which the acoustic element disappears and becomes the highly precise experience of a change permeating my whole body." [15]

Some of these texts have been used previously as material for room installations, performances and audio publications. The rest appear here for the first time. I hope readers of this book will one day feel inspired to be in place somewhere.

Jason Kahn

Table of Contents

October 13, 2011
Brussels, Belgium

Galerie Ravenstein

I arrive shortly after seven a.m. in the rotunda of the Galerie Raven-stein. I enter from Rue Ravenstein above and plunge into the relative darkness of the space, where I'll spend the next ten hours. At first I'm a bit puzzled, everything seems so much darker and run-down than when I was here four years ago. Traffic sounds filter in quietly from the Rue Ravenstein above and from behind, further down the main corridor of the gallery from Rue Cantersteen. A steady current of cool air accompanies the faint morning sounds.

I take a seat on the steps leading up to the first floor of the rotunda and have a look around me: the restaurant Exki already has its tables and chairs out, and a few early birds have stopped there for a quick coffee before heading off to their offices. Fashion Food, Exki's main competitor and the only other business on the ground floor of the rotunda, is still closed. A trickle of people enters from the Central Station down behind me, and they make their way up the stairways to Rue Ravenstein. Sounds waft around me, I can't seem to locate their source. Up above on the second floor and closed off to the public, the Center for Fine Arts Brussels has its offices and a cafeteria for its employees. They use metal chairs and tables up there and occasionally these screech across the stone floor, sounding like some prehistoric birds disrupting the new day's tranquility.

Aside from the morning cold and my still being a bit drowsy, the rotunda creates a comforting atmosphere. Like being submerged in a warm bath of sound. Indeed, over the day I'll keep returning to this idea of being immersed in a huge tank of water. I envision the space getting inverted, with spectators looking in from the empty shop windows into the rotunda, filled now with water and dolphins or colorful fish, rekindling memories of family trips to Sea World or the Monterey Aquarium. But the only place where there might have been water here is the dry and cracked fountain in the middle of the rotunda. Painted a light blue and decorated with embossed palm leaves – a nod to some colonial reminiscence, I guess – I can't picture the fountain having held water for years. The strange thing is, most people passing through the rotunda walk respectfully around the empty fountain, as if it still held water or perhaps just in deference to its former glory.

An elaborate mosaic of half-inch tiles covers the floor, the walls and the eleven columns towering the length of the rotunda's height. I feel like I'm in some giant Turkish bath and the effect is not dissimilar: sounds constantly swirl around, build, achieve an incredible density and then miraculously evanesce into the heights of the glass dome above. At times this all feels like a psychedelic sound experiment, not only sonically but also spatially perplexing.

Walking around the ground floor of the rotunda I listen for all the areas of reflection, moving towards the middle, back towards the walls. Sounds seem to be clearer the further away from the center I move. Going up the stairs the body of sound begins to thin out, as if in direct relation to the growing intensity of daylight cascading in from the glass roof above. Moving towards the entrance to Rue Ravenstein feels like crossing a raging river, with light and sound and cool air pouring in from the street above. The mood is brittle and harsh up here and I head back down to the relative warmth and hospitality of the rotunda's ground floor.

By nine a.m. or so a continual parade of people bustles through the main hall and up the stairs of the rotunda. It's astounding how little they talk, the sound of their scurrying footsteps fills the space, the occasional high heels clicking like machine gun fire up the stairs or across the tiled floor to the entrance of some offices located in the rear of the rotunda. All this sound hangs like a clinging gray mist in the space, arousing memories of navigating foggy streets in London. The door of Exki ruptures this morning sound field every couple minutes or so, as it swings closed with a dreadful crack. At first this bothers me but I soon learn to live with it, even this sound of disruption finding its place in the balance here. Occasionally, one of the restaurant workers will try to prop the door open, but within moments an indignant customer slams it shut again. This will go on and on until the rotunda starts to warm up with morning sunlight and no one minds leaving the door open.

Around ten a.m. the morning rush hour seems to be over and a hush settles over the rotunda. Individual sounds become more discernible now, even sounds from outside the gallery making themselves present: a police siren, a large truck moving slowly by, cars honking their horns. And voices from the top floor trinkle down like light rain: a laugh, a salutation, someone sneezing. All of a sudden, like a wave gaining momentum on the horizon, a troop of school children starts marching up the main hall of the gallery. They enter the rotunda with squeals of laughter, screaming, shouting, the teachers barking out orders in turn. The whole cavalcade like an imploding train of sound snaking its way through the gallery. As they reach the upper floor, their peals of laughter sound like bells going off and before I know it, they've vanished out onto the street above. With them gone, the silence in the rotunda swoops down like a demolishing hammer blow. It's as if all these kids' voices have swept the rotunda clean of its sounds, leaving a yawning vacuum behind them.

I'm back sitting on the stairs now, staring across the sea of tiles spread out before me: every now and then, among the blue, yellow and beige patterns, a small red tile punctuates the space, most of the color long since rubbed away on the tiles nearing the center of the hall, those along the wall still a bright crimson. I don't even want to know the work that went into doing this. It's absolutely insane. Looking up I see a boy and a girl with sound recording equipment. Now, this was something I wasn't prepared for. I mount the stairs and attempt to casually saunter by. The boy eyes me suspiciously. I walk over to the other side of the rotunda. They spend around ten minutes making a recording then move back down to the ground floor and do the same. I guess it's not that interesting for them, though I can't for the life of me imagine why not. But then, they probably couldn't in their wildest dreams appreciate why I would find it so interesting to spend ten hours standing around here all day doing nothing. Maybe I don't really understand this myself, either.

And the strange thing is, no one seems to pay me any mind. Or at least they politely refuse to acknowledge my existence. Not many people loiter here: the occasional homeless person, maybe someone stopping to make a phone call or sit down for a minute to read a map or newspaper. Virtually no tourists arrive – which is fine by me – and only very rarely does anyone stop to look at the space or snap a photo. I start to feel sorry for the rotunda, it seems to have been forgotten or perhaps never even discovered in the first place. All its grandeur has slowly decayed, its stores stand empty, travelers dash through every morning and every evening but none of them prizes the intricate tile work, the wonderful acoustics, the body of light showering down from the glass dome above.

At midday the tempo picks up again, the office workers make their way to Exki and Fashion Foods for lunch. Pretty soon all the tables in front of these restaurants are filled, the rotunda surges with the sound of conversation, percolating up from the ground floor and colliding with the same lunchtime rhythm in the cafeteria of the Center for Fine Arts up on the second floor. That light and airy feeling from the morning is gone now. The sound is compact, compressed, taught, like a monstrous block distending outwards to fill every nook and cranny of the rotunda. I walk from the ground floor to the first floor, trying to find some respite from this onslaught, but everywhere I go it seems the same, just this one impenetrable field of pulsating sound.

Within an hour or so most of the workers have returned to their offices. It feels like the rotunda is now digesting all this sound which it has gorged itself on for lunch. I think of this space feeding off the sound its visitors bring each day, for if they won't show this grand old hall their appreciation they can at least contribute the sound of their voices and motion. I walk again slowly around the perimeter of the ground floor, savoring this new lull in the day's rhythm. Standing in front of one of the abandoned stores I abruptly hear voices. It sounds as if someone is talking right over my shoulder. I turn around and look into the store: only darkness, not a person inside. And also nobody near me in the space. This brings back memories of being in the Gol Gumbaz tomb in Karnataka, India, where one can send whispers around the interior wall. Does the rotunda of the Galerie Ravenstein work the same way? This could hardly be possible, but all day I've felt this disassociation from sounds and their sources, with suddenly a voice or a scrape or some indistinguishable noise raining down on me, murmuring over my shoulder, appearing before me like a visitation from another world. I guess I must be hallucinating at this point, punch drunk from too many hours spent in this churning turmoil of sound. I'm losing my bearings.

And then three teenage boys suddenly careen up the stairs behind me, hooting and hollering, just like my kids do when we're hiking up in the Alps and want to hear the way their voices echo back from the stone ridges around us. But these kids' voices don't echo, they ring out like an anarchic pinball machine gone berserk, with electric vectors of sound zigzagging back and forth from wall to wall, ceiling to floor. They slice the air of the rotunda into pieces. It's exhilarating and I find myself wanting more of the same.

The sun has finally broken through the clouds and fierce white light fills the rotunda. And now I'd like to hear something analog to this brilliant luminescence: even more kids screaming, sirens and horns and a thousand secretaries in high heel shoes and every metal chair and table screeching across the stone and tiled floors of the rotunda. But no, the three boys are gone as rapidly as they appeared. The sun withdraws again behind a patch of dark cloud and the gray cap of the glass dome above bears down slowly, filling the space with a somber silence, not unlike a mausoleum.

As I'm getting ready to leave around five p.m., droves of workers enter the rotunda from the Rue Ravenstein above. They scurry and dart to make the trains waiting for them below in the Central Station. Like in the morning, their shuffling feet and occasional voices fill the space, though maybe now there is more laughter for their work day is done and they can go home. And I guess I should go too.

Daitoku-ji

*As I enter the grounds of the Dai-
toku-ji temple complex I hear morning bells ring from two of the sub-
temples. I walk over to the stately
Hon-do and sit down on its front
steps. The building is still closed
from the night. Behind me now a
priest starts to chant, accompanied
by intermittent bells and the even
cadence of a large drum. Roosters
and ravens seem to welcome the*

drums and bells and voices, as they crow and sing along, their morning cries rising well above the din.

Outside the temple, Kyoto seeps in. Sirens and motorbikes compete with the temple sounds and birds. I hadn't anticipated this much going on so early in the morning, but it's truly noisy and rips me out of my half-slumber, one part of me still back home in bed, another part sitting here on the hard stone steps and shivering in the cool morning breeze. A bright light to the left of me illuminates the front of the Hon-do and pierces the darkness like the loud birds and sirens. Strange shadows from the venerable gnarled pine trees guarding the entrance to the Hon-do lunge out before me like prehistoric spiders crawling menacingly across the ground.

I close my eyes to listen. Slowly, Kyoto's sounds recede into the background and the temple fills its own space, screening the city out. When I open my eyes the temple grounds are now bathed in a dim, early morning light. The sirens are gone, the temple sounds and roosters and crows stopped. No other birds have woken up yet and Daitoku-ji is quiet. I close my eyes again, trying to hear all the small sounds in this apparent silence. A light breeze rakes through the many pine trees. The sound reminds me of fine sandpaper chafing the air and provides one more subtle layer to the low drone of Kyoto outside.

A jolting clank of metal and wood wrenches me out of my deliberation. I look over my shoulder and a man has come to open the main doors to the Hon-do. He doesn't seem to know I'm here. The doors fold out to reveal the dark hall within. I walk over to have a look inside. In the early morning light I can just barely make out the sublime golden Buddha sitting on a lotus leaf in the center of the hall. The room is absolutely still, like a vacuum sucking all invading sounds away. I wish that I could enter but one can only peer from outside, the entrance is barred.

I go back to the steps in front of the Hon-do. With the sun up and the temple lights gone I feel as though I've been transported to another place. All the trees, the surrounding temples, the walkway through the complex – all the details now fully in view. And with this the temple sounds grow. The birds are now awake and singing and morning walkers and joggers and people with dogs start to appear, the sound of their advance becoming louder as they walk towards the Hon-do.

Many of these morning people come over to the Hon-do, climb the steps and bow to the Buddha. Sometimes, they toss a coin in the wooden collection box. It takes me a good while to accustom myself to this unsettling collision of wood and metal. Sounding at first like something falling apart, as each coin ricochets back and forth to the bottom of the box. I feel a bit strange sitting there as these people pray, but no one seems to pay me any heed. Or perhaps they're just ignoring me, yet another bothersome tourist in this city of so many tourists.

I no longer hear the surrounding city at all now. Daitoku-ji is in full bloom, a world unto itself. If I really try, I can pick out details from Kyoto outside, but it's almost like I have to wrestle these sounds from Daitoku-ji's grip. It's not that the temple blocks these outside sounds out as much as it fills its own space with so much sound. Though now the birds have piped down and the drums and bells are gone, Daitoku-ji seems more full than ever.

A very shrunken old man slowly makes his way to the stairs leading up to the Hon-do. He's so hunched over that I can't believe he sees much more than the ground beneath his feet. A walker supports his two hands as he inches forward. At the base of the stairs he leaves the walker and now – unbelievably – walks up the stairs to the entrance of the Hon-do. I've stopped watching him now. I hear the clank of the coin thrown in the collection box, followed by a slow and deep, almost imperceptible chant. And then in an instant his chant turns into a song and he has the most beautiful voice. This goes on for quite some while and I'm thinking the whole time, "Oh, I wish I could record this ... damn!" And then it occurs to me that I am recording this, sitting here and imprinting the sound of his voice in my memory, just as this whole day will also be permanently ingrained in my memory when I turn to go home. What's the point of a microphone?

Another old man arrives, tosses his coin in the box, genuflects to the Buddha and then goes to one of the wooden struts supporting the branches of the aged pine tree still flourishing in front of the Hon-do. He knocks several times on one of the struts and then places his ear to the wood, as if he can hear its soundness or judge the health of the tree by listening for the pulse of its sap. The "chock chock chock" of his hand striking the wood sounds very satisfying and I can well believe that he's been doing this every morning for years now.

I close my eyes again. The odd car, motorbike or bicycle bumping across the stone walkways of Daitoku-ji appears, mixed with the sound of dogs growling or barking and the gait of morning joggers tap-tap-tapping across the stones or dragging through the gravel, which covers most of the temple grounds. A woman's voice calling "ohayo" jolts me out of my revery. I call back to her, "ohayo," and then, much to my chagrin, she is shortly joined by five other women. They start to do their morning gymnastics together, right in front of the Hon-do! It's such a ridiculous sight that I close my eyes again, but then they start to sing together, a kind of soft counting, very melodic and also entrancing in its own way – a stark contrast to how the women look, decked out in their garishly colored jogging suits! The singing stops and I hear their voices now, talking discreetly, laughing. They've finished and as I open my eyes again they're already gone.

I've been sitting at the Hon-do for several hours now and decide to get up and exercise my legs and have some tea over at the rest house. The crunch of the gravel under my feet as I walk away from the Hon-do sounds like a flurry of small bombs going off. I have to readjust to this new perspective, away from the whispering pine trees and the jarring coins of the Hon-do.

After having some tea and breakfast I move on to the Sentai-Jizo, one of the other places I'd chosen in the Daitoku-ji compound for this day. Resembling a kind of graveyard, though in fact not one, the Sentai-Jizo lies secluded behind some tall shrubs. Unlike the Hon-do, not many people pass by here. I take a seat on the cold stone bench in front of the row upon row of Jizo statues. I hear more of the city from this vantage point, the Sentai-Jizo being in line with the east entrance gate to Daitoku-ji. I can hear people walking by beyond the bushes hiding the Sentai-Jizo. Children are now on their way to school. Their whoops of joy fill the morning, along with a very bright sun already shining overhead.

A man enters the Sentai-Jizo and bows to me. "Konnichiwa," he calls. "Konnichiwa," I reply back. Again, I feel like an intruder here but the man seems very friendly. He is the caretaker of the Sentai-Jizo. He turns on a water tap and places a plastic bucket beneath. The sound of water filling the bucket could just as well be a plunging waterfall to my ears, so violently does the water wrench apart the serenity of the Sentai-Jizo. As the bucket slowly fills, the man collects all the porcelain tea cups placed in front of the Jizo statues and washes them out in the water. The cups click together, creating a nice contrast to the trickling water. I start to feel as though I'm audience to a private concert, as performed unbeknownst for me by this man. After washing all the tea cups the man takes a wooden ladle and throws water over the Jizo statues, rinsing away the previous day's dust and nurturing the many clumps of moss thriving there. Water slaps brightly across the many stone figures. I close my eyes again and listen to the intermittent gush of water from the tap into the bucket, followed by the dousing of the Jizo statues. This goes on for some time until I hear, "Arigato gozaimasu," whereby I open my eyes and the man is bowing to me from the entrance to the Sentai-Jizo. I reply in kind, "Otsukaresama deshita," and bow my head. The man leaves.

I drift away in the time passing, the coming and going of people beyond the Sentai-Jizo. The sun burns now from the west, flinging long shadows across the ground in front of me. Nobody has entered the

Sentai-Jizo since the caretaker left. Occasionally I hear a piano playing, then some marching music, a voice on the radio, and when the wind is just right, class bells from a nearby school. I move back to the Hon-do and all these sounds disappear. Here birdsong fills the air, with the recurring herd of tourists passing through, my ears straining to hear if I can understand their language. Their cameras click off, the pages of their guide books turn, they "ooh and ah" at the big golden Buddha, the incredibly gnarled pine trees, the sheer immensity of the Hon-do, so old and solid and seemingly indestructible.

As the sun slowly flags in the west a strong wind kicks up, blowing fiercely through the trees. The branches full of pine needles amplify these shafts of wind, make them visible as the trees pitch and shiver in the warm currents of air. Each squall seems to erase all other sounds in the temple grounds. And when the wind stops the temple fills again with the din of the city outside, slowly regaining its ground as daylight fades.

A bell from the tower behind the Hon-do cloaks Daitoku-ji in its sound. It seems to take forever between each strike of the bell. Just when I think the sound has stopped the priest strikes the bell again. This goes on for some time and then, finally, it doesn't ring again, the last reverberations from the old bell dwindle in the gathering dusk and also mark for me the end of this long day at Daitoku-ji.

Shibuya Crossing

Clambering up the stairs from the Tokyo metro, I feel as though I've arrived at the wrong place. The sprawling intersection in front of Shibuya station has never sounded this way to me before. Agitated masses of hungry crows swoop down on the mounds of trash lying everywhere. Their grim cawing fills the cool morning air, oscillating back and forth across the formi-

dable intersection. Traffic is light. A few cars and the odd cyclist moving nearly soundlessly through the crossing. Four commanding video screens in varying degrees of grandiosity perch black and silent over several buildings on the opposite side of the intersection. I've never seen these screens turned off before, their kaleidoscopes of color normally lording over the area, each screen aggressively competing for every passerby's undivided attention and saturating the area with an impossible web of tangled sound and light.

The relative peace and quiet totally confuses me. The odd early morning bus barges through the silence with a blast of diesel exhaust and loud air horn. Last night's sagging bar denizens straggle towards the metro entrances, some laughing, some puking, some crying, painfully disentangling themselves and making their way home. Their subdued farewells of "bye bye" feel like a cool breeze to my ears and it gradually dawns on me that I've accidentally stumbled upon some vacuum point in Tokyo's overwhelming density. The city looms around me but I don't actually seem to hear it. Its being presses down on me as a solid body of sound and light and smell.

I hear the pigeons now. They coo placidly, barely recognizable above the increasing low frequency rumble of the city waking around me. To my right a train crosses a steel bridge and sends deep, ominous tremors through the ground. Feeling the sidewalk shake beneath my feet ushers in a sudden fear of Tokyo's earthquakes. Trash collectors make their ill-humored debut. Their black plastic brooms whisk across the stained concrete, scratching up small bits of paper here and there. Like little explosions, their dustbins open and close with a violence that belies their size. As a trash truck arrives, the crows shriek with fury at the threat of losing their breakfast. Men leap from the trucks, emptying the spewing bins and carting away the stinking bags of trash. The grueling sound of the trucks compressing all this refuse marks the day's beginning. Traffic slowly builds but everything is still mysteriously quiet, perhaps just a long sigh before all hell breaks loose.

At nine a.m. the sleeping video screens go on abruptly with a whopping burst of sound and light, shattering the morning quietude. Time for business! The screens compete with each other, alternatively louder, at times syncing for a brief respite of unity promoting an upcoming fashion show, then splitting up again into a babel of television personalities, pop stars, pleas for charity, pitches selling chocolate bars, even the screens advertising themselves, boasting of their size, their importance. The images on the screens barely shine through the glaring morning light, though the sheer vehemence of their sound easily makes up for this. It all seems a bit sad, as there is hardly anybody around to hear them yet, stare up at their fast-moving images and gaudy colors. The crows have now fled, perhaps scared off or discouraged beyond all hope by this daily intrusion of their space.

The perspective of the crossing now stretches back and forth in direct relation to the loudest screen, tugging my ears this way and that. The space is elastic and dissected by the sound of the screens. I cross the intersection to the smaller of the screens. I hear it loud and clear now and the trains crossing the bridge to my right fairly roar as they enter and leave the station. Walking back across the street to the empty space in front of the Tokyu department store, the larger screens tilt back into focus and the amassing influx of commuters emptying out of the JR station adds a new layer of texture to the expanding block of sound. I begin to feel as though I'm in a pressure cooker, experiencing sound as something substantial and resilient and menacing. The four main sources of sound – the commuters, the video screens, the traffic and the trains rumbling above ground – all build off each other, vying for control, a pendulum of sound mounting with each stoplight, each arriving train. And the occasional blacking out of all four screens for twenty to thirty seconds offers only some brutal respite, because when they go back on again the screens always seem that much louder than before. I move slowly from corner to corner of the crossing but now the sound seems uniformly repressive everywhere I go.

At some point earlier on in the morning I closed my eyes and dreamt the crows were seagulls and the congested traffic whitecaps breaking on the shore. It is now midday and when I close my eyes I can only hear the crossing for what it is: a supersaturated cacophony of sound and image battling for preeminence. Still, considering the sheer number and density of people moving across the intersection, there is a strangely collected aura of calm at play here. I don't hear cell phones ringing, or people speaking loudly. Even the click-clack of women in high heel shoes rarely breaks the monotony. This bizarre tranquility is more unsettling for me than the imperious video screens and the snarled traffic. I long for some chaos.

The rude, tinny blare of a distorted voice barking through megaphones mounted on a large black truck covered in Japanese flags breaks my concentration. The voice stops and something sounding like a Muzak rendition of a Japanese folk song ricochets from corner to corner of the crossing, sound bouncing psychotically from the glass façades of the highrises. Another truck moves slowly across the intersection, advertising the latest Boy Group and playing their hit single at a decibel level designed to crush the politically-charged megaphones of the first truck. The trucks dawdle for a while in the intersection until it perhaps becomes clear that neither one is getting its message across and then both slowly move on. I cross to the plaza in front of the JR station. Two different political groups are preparing for their demonstrations. And behind them, in front of the entrance to the Tokyu department store, a small stage and sound system is being erected. A banner hung above the stage reads, "Shibuya, entertainment city!"

A man from one of the political groups starts his speech, amplified with two megaphones from a small white truck parked behind him. He seems to be complaining about gay people. A woman comes over from the other group and starts screaming fiendishly at him through her megaphone, "Sumimasen, sumimasen, sumimasen!" over and over and over again, completely out of control, her voice climbing in pitch with each iteration of her attempt to stop the other man from talking. Someone from her group comes over and pulls her away. But the other man has never stopped talking, undeterred as if nothing has happened. The woman walks away and her group starts its megaphones, expressing doubt about the reality of Korean "comfort women." A never-ending wave of commuters now oozes like lava out of the JR station and both demonstrations bob under momentarily in the flood of people, surfacing again as everyone moves on across the intersection and dissolves into the jumbled concrete jungle of Shibuya spreading out away from the station.

Some music from the stage in front of the Tokyu department store now makes a sad attempt to be heard above this awesome din. Four young women in matching gold lamé jump suits dance across the stage and sing to a backing track. Even standing right in front of the stage I can barely hear them, especially as now the first truck with all the Japanese flags has parked behind the other two demonstrations and has started to pump up its music at an incredibly loud volume, for a brief moment eclipsing every single other sound at the crossing. Two undercover police officers appear and tell the driver of the truck to turn off his sound. The two other demonstrations continue for a short while longer. Once they've finished, the man in the first truck scrambles desperately to find the right cassette tape, pops it into his deck and makes one last stand at filling the crossing with his venom and foul music. As he pulls away from the curb another truck appears behind, advertising yet another Boy Group with the latest hit blasting from the truck's speakers, loud and garbled.

I need a break from this whirlwind of sound and cross the street back to where I arrived in the morning. Here, under the shade of a tree, I feel somewhat sheltered from the din, if only symbolically as in reality it's not much quieter here. Especially as to the right of me a man is singing to something he is hearing in the headphones from his mobile phone, his own private/public karaoke party. His voice has this incredibly strident nasal quality, cutting through the noise around us like a knife. In the broadest, most benevolent meaning of the word, he can't sing, yet he doesn't seem to care, oblivious to the people staring at him, laughing at him, making fun of him right before his eyes. One homeless man spits in the singer's direction. The air seems incredibly charged with a nervous tension. Eventually a salaryman comes over to the singer, pats him on the back and strikes up a lively conversation with him.

I cross the intersection again and stand below the biggest video screen, its sound engulfing me like a tremendous waterfall, devouring all the trucks with megaphones, the music stage with dancing, singing women, the public karaoke man, the trucks advertising pop groups and pachinko salons, the odd police siren and bus horn, and the trains plodding in and out of the station. In a way, here it is quiet! Here is only the sound of one screen, nirvana, the eye of the tornado, the epicenter of the crossing. What I had so detested in the morning is now my sanctuary, even though my ears are still ringing, my eyes still stinging from the exhaust fumes, the blood in my head pounding from the pressure of so many people, so much sound.

As the sun slowly sets behind the tall buildings, the evening multitude make their way back to the station. The demonstrations have now finally all dispersed. I cross the street, enveloped in a seething cauldron of people. As I enter the station to leave I hurl one last glimpse back at the crossing, at the blinking screens, at the evening lights going on, at this unfathomable mass of sound.

Place Royale

*It feels like the whole world open-
ing around me as I enter Place
Royale, the barest of sounds ricocheting like small thunderclaps
off the buildings surrounding the
square. The cooing pigeons sound
bigger than I've ever heard them,
the hue and cry from the seagulls
surpassing any levels of aggression
I've ever attributed to them. And
perhaps louder than all these*

sounds is the onerous silence of the noble fountain crowning the middle of the square. An occasional drop of water leaking from one of the numerous spigots lands with a resolute plop into the empty stone basins.

Little by little I get accustomed to the wild acoustics of the square and the morning settles down into what passes for quiet. I make a slow surveillance around the square, noticing how even my attempt at walking carefully sends the sound of loud footfall discharging around me. A couple of stragglers from the evening before enter the square from the other side, arguing vigorously about something. After a few rebounds around the square their voices sift away into the soft morning light. A blue sky is just lifting over the eastern horizon as the sun rises above the rooftops surrounding Place Royale.

I go to sit on the lip of the fountain. The square is like a vessel holding a deep pool of pale gray light. And the sound matches this, indistinct, flickering now just beyond recognition and purling delicately around me. The seagulls have for some reason departed, leaving the pigeons to coo unruffled at my feet. Their gently beating wings and deep chattering creates an aural foundation for the square to rest upon.

A small car materializes on the other side of the fountain. Machine noises fill the square. A man gets out of the car and opens a trap door leading to the mysterious bowels of the fountain. He fiddles around with some valves and levers for some time and then, with an amazing clatter, the fountain spurts on to its full brilliance, all spigots exploding with water splattering against bare stone. And then, just as unexpectedly, the water stops. Momentarily rent apart, the morning now folds back in on itself. The birds slowly dare to take up their places again and I too inch back to my seat, having made a hasty retreat as water sprayed all around me and the sound of the fountain shocked me out of my morning reverie. Seemingly satisfied that the fountain works, the man gets back in his car and drives away.

What follows for the next hour or so is a rapid sequence of different machines and city personnel entering the square to spruce it up and make it presentable for this new day. First comes the man with the high pressure water hose, the water hissing like a wicked snake and sending trash skittering away from the fountain and out to the perimeter of the square. Then the vacuum truck arrives. It ambles painstakingly around the square like some foraging animal, inch by inch its voracious maw sucking up the bits of trash, with rotating brushes working like maniacal discs of sandpaper as they scour the pavement clean. And finally, a person without a machine this time comes to retrieve the odd scrap of rubbish that his predecessors might have missed. He flicks the pieces of paper and the occasional plastic bottle into his metal dustbin, which snaps open and shut each time with a menacing clap that pops around the square like a gun going off.

At eight a.m. sharp the fountain turns on again, its entrance this time somewhat mitigated by the previous succession of machines and sanitation procedures. But this time the fountain stays on. I walk closer to admire its industry, pumping so much water through so many spigots, creating so many waterfalls and rivulets. The air smells sweet and a halo of cool humidity encloses the fountain. All this crashing water creates such an impermeable mass of sound that I assume this will color the rest of the day for me. I am both somewhat irritated and amused by this realization but figure that either way I am going to live with this. When the sun comes out and starts to bake the square I will surely welcome the sight and sound of this watery edifice.

A prominent café on the northeastern side of the square now slowly gets itself ready for the day. Workers haul out tables and chairs and umbrellas to shade the customers from the impending sun. Cumbersome steel pedestals to mount the umbrellas in get dragged across the stone pavement of the square. The sound of steel scraping horribly against stone cleaves through the more friendly aquatic offering of the fountain, making the square nearly unbearable for the duration of the restaurant's morning preparations. It sounds as if the whole square is being ripped apart, like all the surrounding buildings were Hollywood backlot façades toppling down from the sky.

Now more people appear in the square, on their way to work, some taking a seat at the café. I'm sitting by the fountain again. It seems now that I no longer register the sound of the water in any conscious way. It has become like the light, just filling the square with its beneficence but not imposing itself in any way. A man sits down next to me and tries to strike up a conversation. I'm so engrossed in my meditations on this place that I find it hard to talk with anyone, which, I admit to myself, is strange as these people too are a part of Place Royale. But finding myself now in the space of conversation completely befuddles me. It's as if I've left the square for this brief moment of verbal exchange. The man wants to know if I believe in God. "Sometimes," I answer. This seems to satisfy him as he and his colleague move on to grill the next person.

The sun has now crept over the rooftops and bathes the fountain in its heat and light. I move on to the periphery of the square, sitting down in the shadows of an optician on the southeast corner. I feel a bit dizzy from the heat and the unending array of people now roving through the square. Today is Saturday and it seems like the whole city is out shopping. Floating magically, nearly indistinguishable above the easy shuffle of feet and fundament of babbling voices, a melody ekes its way into the square. I feel drawn to this music. It pulls me to my feet and I go in search of it, slowly walking around the square, looking around each corner until I finally locate the source: a man playing accordion down one of the side streets. It seems to me that the music sounded better as heard in the square, mixed in with all the other sounds. Standing directly now in front of the source I feel driven back, the music saturating me, tearing me away from the more cordial ambiance of reverberation and burbling water in the square.

I go back to the square again and station myself in one of the last remaining patches of shade. At this distance I can no longer hear the fountain. As in the early morning it is silent, yet now alive and sparkling like a glittering mass of jewels in the hot afternoon sun. Right in my line of sight to the fountain a break dance group sets up a video camera and proceeds to make a film of itself, every few minutes a different person moving in succession to dance in front of the camera. And like the fountain, these dancers too make no sound. They dance without music and in the din of shoppers and tourists even the movement of their feet can't be heard. I imagine them dancing to the sound of the fountain.

I feel fatigue starting to set in. I crouch down in the last remaining slither of shade and watch heat waves rise from the square, making everything shimmer and dance. It feels as if all sound is in me now, filling my head, trumpeting from my ears as if they were loudspeakers and dissipating with the curls of heat beating against the fountain. I see a rainbow emerging in the mist of the cascading waters. The sound of voices and people walking raises an hermetic seal over the square which slowly closes in, creating a pressure of sound and heat and light that pushes me down to the ground.

A hand in front of my face, palm upturned, jerks me out of my thoughts. A woman wants to know if I have any money. I give her a coin and she moves on. On the other side of the square I hear loud voices, people yelling. A fight has broken out. Screams and shouts ring across the square, then slowly dissipate as the group of people moves on down a side street. The café on the square is full now, people at every table. Laughter and conversation, clinking glasses and clattering silverware fill one side of the square, pulling it away from center and creating a lopsided effect. I walk over to the fountain again. It seems that I've never seen a fountain as vibrant and glorious as this one. I walk all around, admiring its many pools and spouts. I drink in its sound now, the most beautiful sound on the Place Royale, masking the hordes of shoppers, the fight, the noisy café. The square has become this fountain. And like the sun suffusing the afternoon sky above, the cascade of water slices through all the sound around it, shrouding this patch of hot stone and concrete in its cool, watery relief.

Shade starts to fill the square again. The sun rests astraddle over the western rooftops of the square. The shoppers are now dissolving into the streets radiating form the square or stopping by the café for dinner. I can no longer make out any distinct sounds. My head is full, everything gyrates around me. I make one more round of Place Royale and then go home.

Seoul, Korea
October 18, 2013

Art Space Mullae

I'm sitting in the ground floor studio of Art Space Mullae. Early morning light falls from the windows facing east. To the west an elementary school slowly fills with arriving children, some laughing, some crying, parents raising their voices in admonishment or support. These sounds penetrate from the world outside, boring through the walls, piercing the windows.

Sounds from inside the studio also appear as I slowly attune to the room's ambiance. Off in the shadows of the studio's southeast corner something buzzes persistently, like a lone insect overstaying its evening welcome. The elevator doors in the lobby open and close with a muted thud. And each time a person walks through the sliding entrance doors to the foyer, a large folding steel panel opening from the studio to the street behind me shudders and quakes. By the end of the day I practically won't even notice this any more.

All at once, I don't hear the children. They've all made their way into the classrooms and school has begun. Every few minutes a train passes by behind the studio, separated by a narrow strip of grass and trees. I sense the deep bass frequencies of the trains shaking the concrete floor of the studio before I actually hear them swooshing by. The slower trains don't make any sound other than just a nearly subsonic rumble. I fancy the sound of a train flying low above and then slowly grasp that it's actually a jet plane. Though the planes never convulse the building like the trains do.

Next to the studio, a large metal shop – one of many in this neighborhood – starts its work for the day. High ringing tones suffuse the studio and I can't tell if they're coming from the room itself or from outside. I finally realize that the machines in the metal shop have started to whir away, reforming a large pipe or sheet of steel. Accompanying this, a frenzied rhythmic disturbance erupts in the morning air and sends deep shuddering palpitations through my feet. A gigantic machine pounds down again and again. I think first of a monotonous, clobbering drum beat but the longer this goes on the more I rule out any drummer being able to play like this.

The fragment of some classical music melody I've heard hundreds of times before, but now can't put a name on, signals a brief recess for the students in the school next door. Before the music has even finished I hear cries of delight and laughter as the children tumble out onto the playground. Their voices completely overpower every other sound in the studio and I find myself transported into the children's midst, as they jump and hop gleefully around me in all their youthful vigor. And before I know what has happened, the music is playing again. The young voices halt and all the other morning sounds slowly manifest themselves once more, coming out from hiding.

In a brief letup of activity the more subtle sounds of the studio take the foreground. I'm swathed in slowly permutating shades of noise, coiling around me like visible trails of sonic vapor. Streaks of bright yellow sunlight bisect the studio's floor and light up little clouds of dust suspended motionless in the cool morning air. A woman's high heel shoes click-clacking across the tiled lobby floor of the Art Space tear me from my ruminations. Two muffled tones and a woman's robotic voice announce the arrival of the elevator. The loud shoes vanish within. I leave my seat and take a slow walk around the studio, absorbing the different perspectives of sound in each part of the room. Coming closer to the folding steel garage doors at each end of the studio I'm able to hear more of the traffic passing by outside. The sounds from the metal shop gain prominence as I pass the eastern windows. And to the west I can hear kids being unruly in their classrooms. The schoolyard's speakers play a different melody now and all the kids come running outside for their midday break.

I move my chair to the far northwest corner of the studio and take a seat. With all this distance now between myself and the passing trains, the metal shop and the school, the sounds permeating the studio from outside take on a more kindly hue, dampened by the expanse of space. The high ceilings give the room a rich resonance and all the sounds creeping in from outside begin to seethe and churn. I'm not sure any longer what my ears are hearing, so much definition has been lost. The passing trains could be a large machine in the metal shop or maybe a truck passing by in the street behind me. Only the sound of a helicopter buzzing somewhere overhead makes a clearly stated entrance. It chops viciously through all the other sounds. A vision of it landing in the schoolyard flashes through my mind, with all the children fleeing, screaming for their teachers. The whir of the helicopter's blades sends all other sounds in the studio ricocheting from wall to wall, ceiling to floor, a tornado of impossible hues and colors and textures and shapes reverberating madly.

I stand up again and move hastily to the center of the studio to regain my bearings. The helicopter purrs obliquely somewhere off in the west, leaving a gaping sea of silence in its wake. It's midday now and the metal shop workers take their lunch break. The school is also quiet and I see the children away in a cafeteria somewhere having a noisy lunch together. My stomach grumbles too. Its gurgling fills the studio's void. I eat a sandwich and enjoy a slowly evolving mix of light whirring sounds, long tones suddenly appearing and then just as suddenly making their exit. Their absence always seems more vivid than their presence. I picture myself sitting in the humongous stomach of the Art Space, with all the strange organic sounds of a digestive system reaching me from the cryptic nether regions of the building. In the cacophony of morning bustle outside I'd missed this wealth of internal sounds. My focus turns back inwards and the world outside shrinks from view. With the sun now straight overhead, beams of harsh white sunlight no longer pierce through the windows. A kinder, softer light now fills the room, matching the totality of droning, thrumming sounds.

But with a walloping boom, the world outside springs back into action once more. A gigantic machine in the metal shop catapults down again. And again. And again. A train races by, the floor bucks and rolls. That snippet of a classical melody bellows again from the schoolyard speakers and a storm of children's voices rises like a tidal wave about to break across the studio's western windows. I brace myself for a gale of sound, which never really comes. With starts and stops the afternoon presses on, swelling with loud machines, screaming children and then dropping down into an intermission of barely perceptible hums from deep within the Art Center. These recurring oscillations between loud and soft, dense and sparse slowly wear me down. The sounds around me take on a weight, a tangible presence, at times filling the room like so many clouds of fantastic gray cotton balls, or colossal slabs of concrete being hurdled through space and smashing against the walls and floor.

By the time the setting sun radiates a warm yellow light through the western windows, I've finally made my peace with the sounds outside. The children are on their way home, tired now from the long day at school. The machines in the metal shop have been switched off. A large object being pulled across the shop's cement floors is the last sound I hear from it today. More trains rumble by but they don't seem to be in any hurry. The Art Center itself is largely quiet now. Only the sporadic robot voice and chimes from the elevator mark any sign of life in the lobby. I take one more slow tour around the studio, in search of every possible aural perspective but everything is so peaceful now, no matter where I stand. Just the occasional kick from some people scaling the walls of the Art Center outside instils the studio with any life. The climbers call to each other now and then, and their dangling ropes whip lifelessly against the windows. As the last rays of sunlight slowly die away, I feel as though I can hear evening tumbling down around me.

Zürich, Switzerland
October 6, 2011

Grossmünster

The Grossmünster looms before
me on this rainy day, wrapped in
the gray sky and hulking clouds
lumbering out over Zürich's old
city towards the lake. I enter the
church, passing from daylight into
the early morning gloom of the ma-
jestic arches and bare stone walls.
Sound showers down around me and
I feel submersed in a deep, rich,
resonating body. I take a seat

in the wooden pews on the main floor and try to adapt to the relative silence. The day outside leaks in from time to time as a tram passes by, a motorcycle revs its engine, someone sounds their car horn. Soon the small sounds around me manifest themselves, like miniature detonations going off. Every scrape of a shoe, heel and sole stomping across the wooden floors, someone settling into a creaking pew nearby, all these sounds momentarily fill the church with a wrenching violence.

And then the quiet descends again. Silence does not really exist here, but an unmistakable lack of any identifiable sound now hangs over the interior of the church. I hear the blood pulsing in my ears, I visualize the sound of air currents coursing slowly through the church, of everyone's breathing magnified and filling the space like one stupendous breath. The air seems at once to be spinning around me and throbbing with the vitality of all these sounds barely registering in the void. Different hues of gray light pour forth from the ancient glass windows. At times the cavernous room seems to be floating in a murky bath of endlessly permutating light. The glint of a lone candle shines up on the second level of the church, cut adrift in the red and blue light of Augusto Giacometti's stained glass windows.

The church's bells start to ring. They seem far away, as if coming from another church in a distant part of the city. I had assumed the bells would be louder, sound more direct, filling the church with their vibrations. People talking adjacent to me nearly drown out the bells, their voices caroming through the main hall. I get up and walk up the stairs to the second level. Crossing the wooden floor in front of the stairway my steps explode around me, try as I might to tread silently. As I pass under the first arch separating the ground floor from the second level, the acoustics change noticeably around me. Everything seems more controlled, warmer, less the notion of floating in a sea of uncountable sounds. I continue walking towards the very front of the church and take a seat near the wall, directly below one of the two domes.

Off in the distance now, as if a million light years away, the main hall of the church surges with all its activity. It seems very few people come here to pray. Mostly tourists enter the main doors. They talk, their cameras click, they walk heavily over the wooden floors, high heels clicking briskly across the timeworn stone. I guess the Grossmünster is just another place on their itinerary, as most of the tourists don't stay very long. They pile in, gawk at the Sigmar Polke stained glass windows, at the grandiose organ perched on the second level in the rear of the church, at the bare domes and the display of dusty antique bibles in a glass case. Some of the visitors pay to walk up the bell tower and get a bird's eye view of the city. Their voices wash over the main room like tides rushing in and out from sea. A swash of murmurs, laughter, now and then a loud conversation, ebb and flow out on the main floor as I sit under the furthermost dome and enjoy a slim ray of sunlight streaming in through the lofty windows rising up before me.

I walk over to the choir chairs and seat myself there. Here I am closer to the whirling mass out on the main floor of the church. I can see all the people walking in and leaving, milling around in an aimless fashion, lost in the grand heights of the arches, the raw stone, the impression of nearly limitless space sailing way up high in the stirring shadows. For a brief moment, the church seems empty, not a tourist in sight. The silence comes piling down again, nearly taking my breath away. These dramatic spikes in sound levels exhilarate but also wear me down with time, each crest of silence demanding a new orientation to the space.

Out of nowhere I hear a choir singing, just one chord for maybe a few seconds and then they're gone. Why did they stop? Did someone close the door to whichever room they were singing in? Was I just dreaming? I start to feel spooked. Sitting in a church for hours is not without its occupational hazards. The vibe is so heavy here, like a weight pressing down on my body, on my soul. I don't feel at ease. More out of place, distracted by all the sound crackling intermittently around me. I'd like to hear more singing.

Towards midday the gloom begins to lift and a ceaseless mob of visitors swarms in and out of the main doors of the church. I can see this continuing until I leave in the afternoon and begin to dread the coming hours of humanity trampling through these hallowed grounds. The eruptions of small sounds are gone now, just this bewildering miasma of voices and footsteps attaining a standing state of reverberation and agitation. The sense of space when I arrived in the morning is long gone.

I move back down to the main floor and experiment with sitting off to different sides of the room. Yet I soon become distracted wherever I sit, with people always walking by, their voices trailing behind like wisps of smoke. Eventually I return to the middle of the pews, placing myself back in the center of the throng. I feel the room reeling around me, voices sifting up to the limits of the church's soaring heights and dissipating there like vapor. In fact, very few people bother to sit down here at all. They walk about impatiently, looking for some image to consume, some information to read, some memory to take back home with them or to snap up with their cameras.

The accumulation of people here seems independent of any accustomed daily rhythms. It's like the Grossmünster exists outside the normal transition of the day's passing. I slowly get used to this haphazard pacing and decide that perhaps this is what a church is for, to step outside the daily trials and tribulations, take a moment away from the day's course of events and just be still. Which is what I'm trying to do, though I'm certainly not doing nothing: I'm thinking the whole time, concentrating on how I am perceiving the space, thinking about how the sounds here affect how I feel in relation to the room around me, to time slowly passing.

I walk back to the second level and glance upwards towards the dazzling organ, its numerous pipes resplendent with golden angels sounding their horns. Someone has turned on the lights around the organ's keyboard and two men are talking nearby. They go away and then one returns and sits himself down at the organ. I'm not sure what to think about music here, this wasn't part of the equation, as strange as that might sound. And I guess it is strange, because shouldn't music be a part of any church? Shouldn't this have been something to count on, even to look forward to? It seems I was too caught up in analyzing my own perception to allow for the possibility of someone playing the organ.

As I move back down to the main floor again a deep stentorian tone fills the church, as if emanating from the floor below and rocking the main room with an amazing force. Everyone around me stops in their tracks, frozen in disbelief or anticipation. It takes a few minutes before the anonymous organist plays some long slow chords and then a melody. People slowly begin to sit down, as if preparing for an organ recital. This has been the first time today I've seen more than just a few people sit for any length of time, whereas for me the entire day has already been a concert of sound and I've been here the whole time attending it. The more the organist plays the more I think that this sound is an intrusion here. The tones cut through the air, accumulate along the stone walls, snap back and forth from ceiling to floor. The music stops and starts, this is no concert, at least not the kind of concert these people sitting around me had probably hoped for. One by one they get up, return to walking aimlessly around the church, finally leave. The music carries on haltingly. The organist seems to be improvising or perhaps just testing the organ to see if everything is working correctly. There is no structure, no direction, which seems to suit me better. The organ becomes just another intermittent sound, like the clomping shoes, the voices, an occasional noise from the world outside bleeding in through the old stone walls.

Bright afternoon sunlight fills the church. I make one last round from the lower floor to the upper and take a seat again under the last dome. I bask in the intense light and the sound of the organ floats like a cloud off in the distance in the main room. I'm fading away in the warmth of the sun and the rich, deep tones of the organ's longest pipes, barely audible but pervading my chest, as if stemming from some hidden place deep inside my body. Clouds pass before the sun and a momentary darkness fills the church. The organ has stopped too. I make my way through the sea of tourists and head out the main doors to leave.

Zürich, Switzerland
April 21, 2011

Panoramaweg

Zürich opens up before me, stretch-ing out to the north, the sun trac-ing through trees from its horizon in the east. For once I've escaped the sound of traffic. The city rum-bles unperturbed below. I arrive shortly before eleven a.m. and al-most right away the church bells start to go off, seemingly all the churches in Zürich ringing out eleven bells, each church slightly staggered from the other, creating a smear of pealing bells swaying back and forth across the city's basin, swept by the strong winds racing up from the Lake of Zürich and colliding with the slopes of the Uetliberg rising behind me.

Immediately in front of my bench lies a dairy farm, where many cows stand solemnly in their stalls being milked. To the left of this the miserable-looking Hotel Atlantis, probably once the pride and joy of this part of the city, now a home to refugees. And a bit further off to the right, just below the Jewish cemetery, sprawls a seemingly boundless housing development slowly nearing completion. Occasionally the sound of jackhammers and bulldozers reaches my bench, but for once the city seems mostly quiet.

With time I start to determine just how many sounds are in fact present here. The trains traveling up and down the Uetliberg blow their air horns and the track crossings ring their warning bells. I can hear the trains approaching, grinding heavily down their tracks. The birds are ever present, though not in fact as loud as where I live in the heart of the city. And then the jetliners taking off and landing at Zürich's airport. It seems a plane passes nearly every five minutes, but this is probably an exaggeration on my part, the sound of these jet engines is so intrusive. I begin to curse myself for flying as much as I do. The city lies under a virtual net of crisscrossing jets and smaller regional planes, with the occasional helicopter cutting like a chainsaw through the sky. I'm not sure now if I would rather hear cars or planes. Neither, actually, but in this city we have no choice. And some people even live under a flight path.

I'm not sure what I expected to hear up on this ridge. I've been here before, even made sound recordings here before, but never really spent this much time here as I will today. What really makes me listen is the sound of the wind blowing through the trees, like fine sheets of rustling paper. More than any other sound this stands out, different trees trembling above me, in front of me, behind and off to either side. I get the sense of different colors of noise slowly phasing up against each other, like the wind grazing against itself.

People walk by now and then. Mainly elderly, many with small yapping dogs. Most people seem to just look right through me, as if I'm a ghost. Which is fine by me. There is in fact no one else sitting up here, so perhaps it does look a bit strange. Maybe this is what being old will be about one day, just sitting on a bench in some park taking it all in, not even thinking about anything, or at least not thinking about what I'm hearing or seeing or what this all means. Just to sit and listen and look and not do anything else. Maybe when I'm old I'll just stop all this thinking and I won't have to type all these words about me sitting on a bench somewhere.

After a couple of hours a kindergarten files by slowly, kids laughing, some lagging far behind. One little boy has bitten the electrified fence meant to keep the cows in and is screaming bloody murder. His hysterical shrieks of pain cut like a knife through my afternoon idyll. It seems to me in this moment that the sound of a screaming child is the most powerful form of noise known to humankind. Thankfully, they are soon gone, trudging back into the dark reaches of the forest. It takes some time for my ears to recover and follow the sounds around me again. It seems everything has grown louder now, birds I hadn't heard before, multiple construction sites chiming in over the wind, two trains passing simultaneously, one uphill, one down. I must be imagining all this or perhaps this was just timing, everything picking up in the afternoon.

The wind continues to play a maestro's role, modulating the sound of the city below with each mighty gust. It's as if some supernatural being has its hand on a celestial panning knob, slowly twisting the perspective from left to right, at times pushing the sounds right up to the field in front of me, or sending everything flying off to the north, slipping away over the hills into Oerlikon.

I'm trying to imagine the field in front of me from the perspective of an ant, with the sound of all the blades of grass quivering in the wind like so many gargantuan trees. I guess this would be more of a rumble than the benign hiss I'm now hearing. My mind starts to roam with ideas for making this field of grass an auditory phenomenon – a field within this vast field of sound sweeping up from the city and down from the Uetliberg. I'm caught in the nexus between these two sources of sound. At times I feel the Uetliberg practically stooping over me with all its trains and wind and its sombre shadows. And the city vaulting up from below like a wave, reaching out to carry me back to its glistening lake.

The afternoon wears on and the sun begins to wane behind looming gray clouds. Before long it will start to rain. Noise from the various construction sites below seems louder now, as if the workers are trying to push their jobs through before the rain starts to fall. Or maybe I'm just becoming impatient and tired, my senses frazzled from trying to take this all in for so many hours now. I'm beginning to wonder how long I will want to continue sitting here today. The bench is so hard, the wind cuts through my thin pants and I feel like I might be coming down with a cold. And then I see a hawk circling slowly over the field in front of me. He's looking for mice. Another smaller bird flies after the hawk, trying to dive down on to its back. After many attempts he succeeds, only to bounce away in a second and fly on towards the forest, his mission accomplished. "What was that all about?" Probably the most spectacular thing I've seen all day, that and the kid biting the electrified fence. Like the soaring hawk I also begin to feel my spirits lift and I know that I can last for a couple hours more.

I want to sit here until sundown, but I know I won't make it. The wind has picked up and the first drops of rain make their way through the leaves above me. Instead of the wind blowing through the trees I'm now hearing the spatter of many rain drops. And the field of sound around me seems to have folded in on itself, muted by the sound of the rain and the lusterless mat of gray clouds pressing down from above. It's not yet sundown but the day is nearly done, darkness slowly consuming the city below, obscuring the slopes of the Uetliberg behind.

I stand up and stretch, get lost in the rain's now amplified descent on my umbrella. It seems like the wind has stopped. Everyone else with their dogs and kids has gone home for the day. The birds are probably sitting in their trees somewhere, the cows long since back in their barn, and all the laundry which had been hanging out to dry on the balconies and roof of the Hotel Atlantis this morning has been taken down. The Uetliberg train sounds less bright and diligent now, less optimistic about the day. And below Zürich lies in a murky brew of the occasional church bell and nothing more. I head down the hill to catch a train back to the city.

Zürich, Switzerland
May 10, 2013

Paradeplatz

When I arrive at Paradeplatz early in the morning, the sound of the trams pulling laboriously into the square disorients me. I walk around aimlessly for a few minutes, try-ing to find a good place to start my long day here. I decide to sit down on one of the four benches in an alcove just northwest of the square. Several trees surround a large fountain. Three strokes of the bells from the Fraumünster church waft heavily over the morning air. Delivery trucks fill the area around the fountain and benches. With loud clanks of metal the trucks' doors burst open and delivery men noisily roll dollies of food over the cobblestones to the restaurants behind me. A terrific whack signals three men dropping a prodigious cardboard tube onto the street from their truck. All the birds scatter from the trees like a bomb went off. The men then huff and puff as they slowly extract a large carpet from the tube. The manager of the Savoy hotel appears and shows the men where to bring the carpet. He then commences to loudly harangue the hotel's window washer, his voice gravelly and rough. The manager decides to show the window washer how to do his job and climbs a tall aluminum ladder. It rattles loudly as he ascends and takes a squeegee to the windows, squeaking and squealing as he draws rubber across glass. The birds still haven't reappeared, or if they have I can't hear them any longer.

Without warning a long clear tone, something between a bell and an air raid siren, fills Paradeplatz. This goes on for several minutes but I can't locate the source. It seems to fall from the sky like the contours of some immense auricular light capping the area. The tone melts away as instantaneously as it had appeared, like the tide going out and leaving the area to its own sounds: the restful burble of water into the fountain from two spigots; the birds chirping merrily again in the trees; the arriving and departing trams vibrating the ground beneath my feet.

Every three to four minutes a tram enters or leaves Paradeplatz, traveling in one of six different directions. The old trams signal their arrival from afar. They creak and groan under the weight of so much aching steel, with so many people aboard coming to start their work day in one of the banks or stores here around the square. Sometimes these old trams sound broken. Tragic wounded mechanical creatures limping into the square. They squeal to a stop and lurch like a bag of shattered pieces of steel when they leave again. The newer trams glide almost noiselessly to and from their stops. Their doors open with a precision whoosh to street level, affording their passengers an effortless exit or entrance. The older trams spill out their mechanical steps with a loud snap and people struggle to navigate them, heels clanking and knocking, baby carriages hoisted up high, sometimes getting stuck and parents cursing under their breath as they try to extract themselves.

Not far away at the lakeside end of the Bahnhofstrasse lies a harbor, home to Zürich's fleet of ships. I'm pleasantly surprised when the deep, forlorn tone of an old steamer's air horn shoots down the Bahnhofstrasse and ricochets around Paradeplatz. This sound from the past totally surprises me. I feel transported back one hundred years to the time of this ship's construction and see the square then, filled with the sound of horses pulling rattling wagons behind them as their hooves clip-clop across the cobblestones. The high-rev caterwaul of a sports car's engine from the Talackerstrasse at the western end of the square brutally jerks me back to the present and calls to mind that I'm at the epicenter of Switzerland's financial industry and luxury shopping, though it is still far too early for any of the stores or banks to open their doors.

A scooter driven by a man in orange overalls hurtles to a stop not far in front of me. He walks over to the fountain with some tools and, with the turn of a spigot beneath the basin, sets about draining all the water away. The loud rush of water surging away beneath the fountain becomes the focus of my thoughts. With the fountain empty, the man takes a hose and sprays down the area with a high pressure stream of water sizzling across the stone. And to top it all off he now gets a brush and vigorously scrubs the inner surface of the fountain. The birds decamp once again amidst all this noisy commotion. The man packs his tools and speeds away down the Bahnhofstrasse, shifting loudly through his scooter's gears.

I decide to finally venture out into the middle of Paradeplatz, which is nothing more than a tarmac island surrounded by a network of steel rails. A small structure in the middle of the square houses a tick-

84

et office, a public bathroom and two kiosks. I take a seat on one of the benches at the western end of the square. The dogged incursion of trams squeaking across their rails in varying degrees of resistance submerses me in a hypnotic maelstrom of more or less unbroken sound. Unlike when I arrived, the trams don't seem too loud now, and after not too long I hardly notice them at all. It is only when for a brief moment that either no tram is arriving or departing that I remember their movement. These brief lapses produce something more akin to a sudden low pressure zone than a silence. It feels as if the bottom has dropped out of Paradeplatz, that its very substance hangs together with this continuous flow of tram traffic. The ground no longer rumbles, no old steel wheels squall across their tracks. Just the low mutter of voices and footsteps across the pavement. As short as these gaps of relative silence actually are, they seem in their magnitude to last an eternity. As the day progresses, I look forward greedily to the next hole in time and a break from the unforgiving circulation of the city's public transportation.

The morning wears on, bright sunlight fills Paradeplatz. The arriving trams are full of people on their way to work. The passengers disembark but hardly anyone is talking. Even the cell phones don't ring. Perhaps everyone is just lost in their thoughts, contemplating the long day ahead of them. The stores roll up their metal window shades, throw open their doors. Some Chinese tourists make their entry, huddling together and slowly meandering from one end of the square to another. Their voices rise above the surrounding sounds, a language so foreign to this square, overshadowing the soft, melodic swells of Swiss German. As I move around Paradeplatz I also hear French, Italian, Spanish, Portuguese, German and English. A constellation of different nationalities orbits within the boundaries set by the rhythm of the trams.

I take a seat on one of the benches in front of the ticket office. A young boy plays a game on his phone. Tiny blips and beeps subvert my train of thought, competing for their space against the warning bell from a tram nearly running over a pedestrian. These large and small sounds create a tension, my consciousness veering between fore- and background, pushing and pulling. In this rising swell of sound, the bells from the Fraumünster church have all but disappeared. Only with the greatest of effort can I make them out at all now.

Around midday Paradeplatz fills with people and everyone seems to be chatting with each other, talking on their phones, yelling across the square to friends, laughing. A brief respite from the day's work, people are eager to start their lunch. The two restaurants behind the fountain now fill with diners enjoying the warm weather. I hear the clink of glasses and of silverware striking porcelain. A strong wind surges through the trees overhead but try as I might I can't hear the rustling of the leaves. Occasionally, the loud cries of some birds pierce the mass of sound but for the most part I can't detect them. The lunch hour marks a new density of sound on the square. I see myself moving through an infinite field of resonating sound, layer upon layer, a high pressure zone yielding only with considerable resistance as I wander from one end of the square to another. And then, before I know it, the square empties out again, like the water draining out of the fountain earlier this morning. A massive black hole has replaced the sea of voices. I practically lose my equilibrium in this sudden tectonic rift of sound. The sun beats down mercilessly now and I seek some shade under the roof of one of the kiosks. Sitting on a bench there I hover on the verge of sleep as tendrils of heat rise languidly around me and the trams make their way relentlessly around the square. Even the tourists seem to have lost their voices now.

Under the blazing white light and scorching heat of the late afternoon sun, all sound on the square seems distorted and louder than in the cool shade of the morning hours. The rails sound like they're being torn from the ground by each tram rolling by. Every ringing cell phone pierces the air like an ice pick to my ears. I've taken refuge from the heat again under the eaves of the ticket office. Yet, even here sounds settle around me like blasts of white noise. I must be more tired than I thought. I feel the blood pumping ruthlessly in my temples. I hear my own pulse, beating like a crazed drummer keeping time to the cavalcade of sounds vying for my attention.

As the sun sinks over the buildings in the west I decide to make my way out onto the square again. Clots of tourists stand everywhere. I hear Chinese at all points on the square. Again a cool wind blows benevolently through the square and all sound diminishes in the sweep of this soothing draught of air. I keep walking around and around the square, spatializing the mix of sounds in a slow arc from one end to another. People are starting to leave their places of work, waiting for a tram to take them home or out somewhere for the evening. Like at midday the energy of Paradeplatz surges, the sound level rises. The stress of the day evaporates in this sea of voices and the cool, long shadows cast from the buildings as the sun retires below the horizon. Walking away to where I've parked my bike, I hear for the last time today the bells of the Fraumünster church, resonating on the breeze and settling like a gentle veil over Paradeplatz as evening falls.

Zürich, Switzerland
June 25, 2011

Piazza Cella

Sitting down on a bench at the Piazza Cella the first thing that strikes me is the sound of water. Looking over I see a small fountain, water dribbling down from a narrow metal spout into a shallow granite bowl of water with a few cigarette butts and an empty beer bottle floating in it. I'm sitting at the bench nearest the Langstrasse, right next to the fountain and I decide that I don't want to hear this water for the next twelve hours. But what exactly do I want to hear? I looked forward to experiencing many things: music, traffic, screaming voices, shattering glass, people heaving, doors slamming, police sirens. In short, the sound of every red light district I've ever been too, just like this one. But I hardly hear any of this. If anything the Piazza Cella resembles more a quiet park on a Sunday afternoon.

The traffic in the Langstrasse moves by in an uninterrupted progression of listlessly crawling cars. Buses drive down their lane now and then, sucking all sound behind them in a great low pressure vacuum. Police patrols circle monotonously round and round the square, like patient vultures. When the officers bother to get out of their cars to arrest someone it's all amazingly orderly and devoid of any excitement. Not even the junkies and dealers and alcoholics and prostitutes and crazy people raise their voices. Then I remember that noon is probably like early morning for most of these people. They're not yet quite fully revived from the night before. But how many times have I walked by here in the evening and heard nothing but full fledged parties and fights and a roiling sea of boisterous voices filling the Piazza Cella till it seemed like it was going to explode with so much sound?

Two pretty drunk women appear out of nowhere. They hail passersby and comically harass the police, who ignore them, as they ignore all the crazies here who badger them with questions the whole day long. The officers smile, wag their heads, inattentively agreeing with whatever it is these women are telling them. I catch a steady issue of "ja's" and "nein's." The women giggle conspiratorially and falter away down the Dienerstrasse to their next destination.

I'm waiting for the music to start, to fill the Piazza with sound rebounding from the surrounding buildings. The Piranha Bar, The Longstreet, The Lambada Bar, Schweizer Deggen, Bar Locarno 2000, Bar Stella Alpina. There are so many bars here, each with its own signature sound, each a potential source of loud, abrasive music. But they're all silent still, open for business but not yet recovered from the previous night's festivities. My friend Dave lives above the Schweizer Deggen. One night I was making recordings from his window and all we could hear was totally distorted salsa music blaring with a savage ferocity from Bar Locarno 2000 across the street. And therefore I was sure of this, at least one loud jukebox. But so far just the wind, some dribbling water and a couple of drunk, exclaiming women are all I'm left with.

Over time I become aware of the confusing vortex of languages closing in on me: Swiss German, High German, French, Spanish, Italian, British English, Arabic, Turkish, Serbo-Croatian, Portuguese, a couple African languages which I can't place. Even something that sounds like Finnish. These people all gravitate to the Piazza, take a seat, watch the day pass by into night. Some speak in tongues, languages that didn't exist until these people arrived and found a spot here on a bench. Like the big guy in the suede Midnight Cowboy get-up to my right, intently mumbling something utterly incomprehensible to anyone but himself and his own private demons. He seems to know everyone on the square, tries to hug an old long lost friend, kiss a girl who waves to him. No luck, everyone eludes his clasp. He finally throws in the towel, passing out full length on the bench and snoring contentedly, his final contribution to the Piazza's sound pool.

I'm sitting under the only tree on the Piazza now. An old German guy walks by and asks, "Alles klar?" "Ja," I answer. But I'm not getting what I wanted. It's still too quiet. Maybe I picked the wrong day of the week – it's Saturday. Or the wrong time of day – from twelve noon to midnight. Things do tend to pick up here around midnight, but I didn't want to just hear the party. I thought there might also be some guise of a daytime world going on here. Well, maybe not families out for a stroll, but perhaps also not just police, drug addicts and dealers.

After a while I start to feel the Piazza pulsing with all these individual sounds bouncing off the surrounding buildings, creating a standing pool of deafening tumult. Like a slowly whirling pool of water verging on becoming a stagnant puddle, the sound just seems to sit here, cut asunder now and then by a bus sucking through or a distant siren howling somewhere off in the city. After a few hours I begin to feel like I'm on the verge of delirium, concentrating on all the sounds, on all the sights, the people coming and going, the gray sky pressing down, squeezing the sound deep into the asphalt of the Piazza.

Some shouting finally going on in the Schweizer Deggen, of all places. The pressure's building, the clouds are settling in and it looks like rain. Everything slowly takes on a muffled tint, like damp cloth whacking against one of the benches. The police are here again. They just parked near my bench and stepped out of their van. They nod to each other and run across the street to intercept two typical Langstrasse suspects. A stealthy silence envelops the officers as they move efficiently through the traffic. Someone yells out "Hallo …!" The two suspects stop, shrugging their shoulders and looking down at their feet. The clickety-clack clickety-clack of two women in dangerously high heels pans across my stereo field.

These people just come and go. Everyone comes and goes here. I'm the only one who stays. Except for the old German guy, nobody asks me anything. He screams around a bit when two drunken prostitutes try to steal his plastic bag full of beer, concealed none too inconspicuously under his bench and practically begging to be stolen. He teeters off to cadge another cigarette from someone. Maybe I look like a cop, or an idiot, or a crazy, or a damned tourist. Some guy just sitting here all day, twiddling his thumbs, watching the world go by, the sounds sailing by. No, I'm listening, or watching, or just being. What a novel idea, to just sit somewhere and do nothing. Just be there. Take it all in. Start to hallucinate, to feel dizzy with all the detail, all the faces and voices and strutting characters.

After eight or so hours the sound field of the Piazza begins to collapse in on itself. I don't even know what all the sounds are anymore. It all just seems to dangle tightly above my head or drip slowly like drying paint from the blackened windows of the abandoned building next to Bistro Pub Aladin, with its two televisions tuned to perpetual sports channels. I start on a slow elliptical path around the Piazza, from bench to tree, tree to bench, stopping to take a long drought of water from the fountain, persevering bravely in its steadfast gurgle, the one sound unifying the cacophony of the square. I'm starting to enjoy the sound of the water now, it focuses my energies on something I can hold on to, my vantage point in the midst of this intoxicating field of sound. Now more than ever I want the night to come, for each bar to light up, each jukebox to roar. If I try hard enough I can almost hear the barrage of music. My head is spinning. It's fabulous. What a delirious pleasure. What if I sat here for twenty-four hours?

The sky's definitely falling, I can feel a drop of rain now and then. A gray swath of cloud exerting an onerous pressure on the square. The wind's died down and, as they say here, when the wind stops blowing that's when the rain starts to fall. I'm waiting under the tree again. And I hear the pitter-patter pitter-patter of the odd rain drop ricocheting from leaf to leaf. It's getting on to midnight now, and the rain's really starting to stream down. This is all I can hear, that and the unrelenting swish swish swish of the passing traffic. The rain doesn't cleanse away anything, it just turns the dust to mud. I'm getting wet. And I notice that my ears are ringing. Or is that just something going on in my head, like bells going off, or glass breaking? The Piazza is splitting apart, people are groaning. Or is that just thunder? The sky splits in two. At last the finale I'd been hoping the whole day for, a loud boom! ricocheting from building to building around the Piazza. I think it's finally time to go.

Zürich, Switzerland
April 22, 2013

Röntgenplatz

The sound of bulky steel objects rasping across concrete greets me as I arrive at Röntgenplatz this cold, windy and wet morning. Two city workers are in the process of removing one of the three large picnic tables normally left on this large square of gravel. A group of school kids sits on the other tables, their animated voices blown every which way by the wind. As the bells from St. Joseph's church ring eight o'clock, the kids scurry away to make it in time for their first class of the morning. I take a seat at one of the tables situated under a metal shelter installed on one corner of the square. Light rain dances down softly and I shiver in the cold morning air.

The clamor of construction work one street away in the Quellenstrasse dominates the area. Bulldozers, steamrollers and the insistent banging of pickaxes, shovels and hammers cuts through the morning air. In the Fabrikstrasse a team of workers disassembles five stories' worth of metal scaffolding. I catch snatches of Italian, Spanish and Swiss German filling the street. At first I'm a bit dismayed by all these voices from the construction sites but steadily other sounds come into focus around me. St. Joseph's bells signal the first quarter hour after eight o'clock and the rain stops. I move out from under the shelter and walk around the square.

Five streets empty into Röntgenplatz, which once upon a time was a very busy knot of traffic until the local residents petitioned the city to close the intersection and have it paved over. It now serves as a meeting point for the area. Each street opens up to another source of sound. As I slowly walk around the square I pass different nodes of sound driving towards me like thick currents of air, more or less evident depending on the fervor of construction work.

To the south, the Zürich main train station's yard hosts an unremitting procession of trains ambling slowly by. The sound of freight trains rattles and creaks across the wind. The newer passenger trains roll by nearly inaudibly and it seems I can only guess at their sound as I watch them. To the west, more trains pass along an old stone viaduct. With the right direction of wind and a pause in construction work I am just able to hear their wheels rolling heavily over the rails. A bit further beyond the viaduct an interminable column of traffic rolls sluggishly across the Hardbrücke, well out of earshot. In my mind I can hear the pandemonium of countless engines and horns and low bass rumble resonating through the bridge as the traffic grinds its way in and out of the city.

To the east of Röntgenplatz trams trudge wearily up and down the Limmatstrasse. The newer trams move soundlessly, the older ones grind painfully across the rails. About the only sound I don't hear is that of traffic. The odd car drives past the square, either lost in the tight network of streets or searching hopelessly for a place to park. With a loud crash, what sounds like a waterfall of breaking glass tears the morning air apart, momentarily obliterating the sound of construction work. A bit further up the Fabrikstrasse a large truck empties out glass recycling bins into its trailer. Thousands of bottles smash against the hard steel of the truck's trailer. All the birds fly away. A baby in a carriage begins to scream. A dog yelps, scampering between its owner's legs. And then in a flash everything is back to normal. Slowly the birds return and I can hear them singing again. The construction workers put down their tools and tromp back to their work shed, temporarily erected on the northeast corner of Röntgenplatz. Their bulky work boots crunch loudly across the gravel covering the square. It's ten a.m. and some office workers arrive for their morning break. The smell of cigarettes and coffee pervades the square.

It occurs to me now that I've entirely forgotten about the bells from St. Joseph's. In their regularity they've all but subsided completely. Only when I really concentrate on their reappearance can I hear them dolefully pealing out the day's progression. With the brief respite from construction work I can now more clearly hear the trains rolling in and out of Zürich main station. From a supermarket on the southeast corner of the Röntgenplatz I can just make out the small electronic bleeps from its two cash registers. Four flagpoles stand in front of the supermarket. Metal hooks affixed to the ropes running their height clink melodically in the wind against the poles. The postman arrives, riding his yellow scooter. Its two-stroke engine obliterates all the more subtle sounds in the area. Valves and pistons hammer away at each other as the postman makes his way from mailbox to mailbox in front of each apartment house on the square. And by now the construction workers have finished their break and move in a line back across the gravel towards their machines and tools. One worker climbs in a timeworn steamroller parked in the Josephstrasse. Its mammoth diesel engine sparks to life and fills the air with sound waves so low that it seems I feel them before I actually hear them. Pungent diesel exhaust fumes close like a dark curtain over the square.

The rain starts again, this time in earnest. I run for cover under the metal shelter. Ear-pummeling drops of water smash down on the roof, reminding me of a group of kids spraying me with pea shooters. An old man pulls up behind me on his bike. He takes out a can of beer from his bike's basket and sits down at the other table. With a loud, satisfying pop he opens the beer. He takes a long swig from the can and lets loose an enormous burp, which momentarily rivals the rain as loudest sound in the area. I'm shivering now in the cold. The sound of my teeth chattering provides a syncopated counterpoint to the raindrops. I briefly enjoy these excruciating rhythms but I don't like being cold. Before long, the rain lets up. To get my blood running again, I leave the shelter of the roof and move slowly around Röntgenplatz.

I walk around the perimeter of the square, enjoying the sensation of each street's runnel of sound competing for my perception. At each street's entrance I pass through a low pressure zone. The air opens up and sounds from further down that street funnel back to me as I trace the circumference of the square at a leisurely gait. At eleven a.m. the bells from St. Joseph's continue on for many minutes after ringing the hour. They compete with the jackhammers, which do their best to keep pace with a bulldozer digging up the Quellenstrasse. A delivery truck parks in front of the supermarket and sounds its air horn. A platform opens from the back of its trailer and whines loudly as it lowers to ground level, laden with boxes holding many glass bottles tinkling from the movement. Magnificently now the sun appears. I shade my eyes from the blinding white light. The warmth feels good.

It's now midday. School kids fill Röntgenplatz again, making their way home for lunch. The construction workers put down their tools and turn off the engines to their vehicles. In the sunlight now everyone seems happy. Birds singing, kids laughing, a bicycle bell sounds warning as its rider moves too quickly across the gravel. I take a seat on one of the benches in front of the supermarket and eat my lunch. The benches slowly fill with people. Inside the supermarket the cash registers beep furiously as long lines of shoppers wait to purchase their groceries. The smell of sausage frying in the construction workers' shed on the square wafts across the air. Birds chirp at my feet as they scurry after crumbs of bread thrown to them by people eating. I hear people talking and laughing all around me.

A brief window of time exists between when everyone has left Röntgenplatz after their lunch break and when the construction workers have gone back to work again. An oppressive vacuum of near silence fills the air. Even the birds have stopped singing. I slowly navigate my way around the square. I hear people talking somewhere in the air above me. Looking up I see two women on a balcony. Their voices spiral down like thin smoke. A whirring sound slowly creeps across my field of hearing. I walk around the square twice before I discover its source: someone tidying up their apartment with a vacuum cleaner. Its nasal drawl undulates lightly, barely making itself heard above the city's deep drone.

I now move to the center of the square, allowing all these small sounds to mix together, phasing in and out with streams of light wind blowing from the different streets, all of which used to converge at the point I'm standing at now. With a rain of shouts and what sounds like an avalanche of boulders slamming into the ground, the construction work begins again. The balance of sound across the square now hangs unevenly, pulled by the severe blows and shouts and the whirring racket of machinery to my left in the Quellenstrasse. I take a seat on one of the stone benches facing southeast across the square. In the street behind me a Sri Lankan food market does brisk business. I hear music from Bollywood films, loud haggling and the battered door to the market swinging back and forth in the wind.

For one fleeting moment, the delicious smell of exotic spices curls enticingly in the air.

Following the sun's trajectory around the square, I sit down once more on a bench in front of the supermarket. It's late afternoon. Kids appear again, coming home from school. Some stop to play, scattering around the area with their bikes and soccer balls. The number of cyclists crossing the square increases now too. Their bells ring in the air, prompting the kids to get out of the way. A group of mothers and babies arrives at the picnic tables. The mothers talk excitedly, the babies cry. The sun blazes down bright and strong. Scores of pigeons and sparrows peck around the gravel on Röntgenplatz, looking for crumbs. The beautiful fluttering sound of a flock of birds taking flight suddenly fills my ears. Voices talking from a radio sprinkle down across the square from an apartment's open windows.

The construction workers call it a day. Their voices fill Röntgenplatz. People sit at every bench, at every picnic table. Bikes whir this way and that, gears changing, bells ringing, brakes howling. Avoiding a near collision, a bike rider cries, "Sorry!" A soccer ball smacks against the wall of an apartment building, then lands with a loud splash in the fountain on the northwest corner of the square. Someone calls my name. It's my friend Edward. He asks me what I'm doing and I tell him, "Working." He laughs and waves goodbye. And I'm surprised at how strange my own voice sounds. It seems like a good moment to go home. The bells of St. Joseph's ring out seven times.

Notes

1   Maurice Merleau-Ponty, *Phenomenology of Perception*,
    New York: Routledge Classics, 2002, p. 404.
2   Henri Lefebvre, *Rhythmanalysis*, London: Continuum,
    2004, p. 30.
3   Ibid., p. 19.
4   Ibid., p. 87.
5   Gaston Bachelard, *Dialectic of Duration*,
    Manchester: Clinamen Press Ltd, 2000, p. 18.
6   Henri Lefebvre, op. cit., p. 73.
7   Ibid., p. 26.
8   Charles Mingus, as told to Nat Henthoff,
    Mingus Lives, Online Wall Street Journal, 2012.
9   Maurice Merleau-Ponty, op. cit., p. 28.
10 Henri Lefebvre, op. cit., p. 2.
11 Maurice Merleau-Ponty, op. cit., p. 301.
12 Henri Lefebvre, op. cit., p. 22.
13 Maurice Merleau-Ponty, op. cit., p. 406.
14 Henri Lefebvre, op. cit., p. 36.
15 Maurice Merleau-Ponty, op. cit., p. 264.

Jason Kahn
In Place

ISBN: 978-0-9889375-4-3
Published by Errant Bodies Press:
Audio Issues Vol. 6
www.errantbodies.org
Berlin & Los Angeles, 2015

Designed by Hille Haupt
Printed at druckhaus köthen
Distributed by DAP, New York

*Many thanks to Tim Olive
for his feedback and sharp eye!
– JK*